Happy Holidays and best wishes for a happy 2023!

Your friends from the FORWARD study

Ann & Robert H. Lurie Children's Hospital, Chicago
Cincinnati Children's Hospital Medical Center, Cincinnati
Rush University Medical Center, Chicago
Children's National Health System, Washington DC
Chicago Family Asthma & Allergy, Chicago

Lancaster, PA
Copyright ©2022 by JJ Vulopas and Riya Jain. All rights reserved. Except as permitted under the United States Copyright Act of 1976, no part of this publication may be reproduced or distributed in any form or by any means, or stored in a retrieval system, without the prior written permission of the authors. This is a work of fiction. Any similarity between the characters and situations within its pages and places or persons, living or dead, is unintentional and coincidental.

Written by JJ Vulopas & Riya Jain
Illustrations by Bill Dussinger
Printed in the United States of America

ISBN: 978-0-9993845-3-4

For information:
Citizens Of Can, LLC
1060 Manheim Pike
Lancaster PA 17601
717-205-3856

jj@thelandofcan.com
www.thelandofcan.com

Today is Can Day.

In our classroom, **every day is CAN DAY!**

My name is Collin, and I am a kid from the Land of Can!

I know.

I do.

I am.

I CAN.

Typically, I'd be excited to go to school, especially on a day like today. Our class is writing a book, and we've been brainstorming ideas!

But last night, before I went to bed, I started to worry.

You see, I had a wild idea for the book: I wanted my pet fish, Gil, to be the main character.

"But what if my class thinks my idea is silly?" I worried. "A talking fish?"

"What if I'm not as clever as I think?"

"What if I spell a worrd wrong when writing?"

One "What if..." led to another "What if..." led to another "What if..." led to a...

Luckily, I've learned some tricks I can use to break free from my Worry Web.

So this morning, even though I was worried, I decided to go to school after all. I'm really glad that I did.

"It's book day! It's book day!" my teacher Mrs. Can shouted as my classmates arrived and found seats in Can Corner. "I'm so excited to hear your ideas! This could be one of the most important books you've ever written!"

"What will it be about?" asked Kayla.

Mrs. Can smiled and reached into her bag. "It will be about…"

We all knew to start the drumroll. We *tap-tap-tapped* our hands on the carpet.

"… ALARMS!" Mrs. Can shouted, pulling a giant alarm clock from her bag. The drumroll stopped, and we went silent.

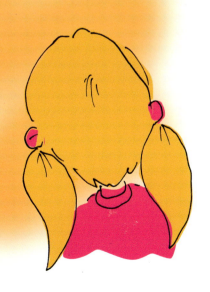

"Alarms?!" Jack whined. "How are we supposed to write a whole book about alarms?"

"Well, not an alarm like this," Mrs. Can laughed. "The alarms inside our bodies! Our Worry Alarms."

"Worry Alarms?" Alex questioned.

"Our Worry Alarms ring when we worry," Mrs. Can explained. "When they're working correctly, they keep us safe! But when they won't stop ringing, we have to learn how to fix them."

The clock started ringing. It didn't stop. In fact, it was getting louder and LOUDer and LOUDER.

Over the ringing, Mrs. Can shouted, "Today, we are going to learn about worry and anxiety!"

"I've heard about worry," Maya shouted. "But what's anxiety?"

"Everyone experiences 'worry,'" Mrs. Can explained, "but anxiety is when you worry so much that you can't turn off your Worry Alarm. It affects what you think, feel, and do."

"Raise your hand if your Worry Alarm has gone off before," Mrs. Can said.

At first I didn't want to raise my hand, but when I looked around, EVERYONE had their hand slowly creeping up. Since I knew I wasn't alone, I raised my hand proud and tall.

FINALLY, the ringing stopped.

"There are lots of things we can do when it's hard for our Worry Alarms to turn off," Mrs. Can explained. "That's why we're writing this book!"

Mrs. Can started to play music from Jamming Jukebox, and we set to work on our book!

Ava and Jack designed helpful posters, Kayla was drawing illustrations faster than lightning, and Maya helped me write the words.

"This is collaboration in action!" Mrs. Can cheered.

We presented the book to Mrs. Can, and she loved it!

I'm excited to show it to you now:

What If?

Words and pictures by the students of Mrs. Can's Class That Can

I don't want to go to school today.

What if I trip and they all shout "Hooray!"

What if I fail?   What if I miss?

What if?

What if?

What if?

What if no one talks to me?

What if I do good but nobody sees?

What if I cry?
What if I slip?

What if?

What if?

What if?

What if at recess no one wants to play?
What if I say "Please!" and they all scream "No way!"

What if I get tired?
What if I get sick?

What if?

What if?

What if?

I don't want to go to school today.
What if at lunch, I drop my tray?

What if I choose A but the answer is B?
What if I shout "B!" but the teacher says "3!"

What if my ideas aren't creative enough?
What if I try to help but mess everything up?

What if I turn left, and others turn right?
What if I walk in and they turn off the light?

What if my classmates don't want to share?
What if I fall going down the stairs?
What if no one likes me? Maybe no one cares.

What if?

What if?

What if?

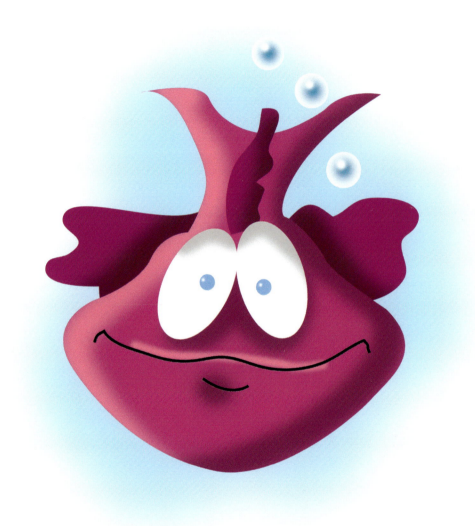

Before we continue, before we hit next,

I'm going to tell you what you should expect.

We could sit here repeating "What if?" all day,

But that would stop laughter, and learning, and play.

How do we make the
"What ifs" go away?

The same way the
nighttime turns into
the day!

Instead of a minus,
make it a plus!
Wonder and vision
lift us UP UP UP!

One thing we can do, one thing that I've found,
Is reverse the "What if"
Flip it all upside down!

I WANT to go to school today!

What if I have fun? What if we all play?

What if my day is a-ok?

What if?

What if?

What if?

I WANT to go to school today!

What if boldness leads the way?
What if they hear what I have to say?

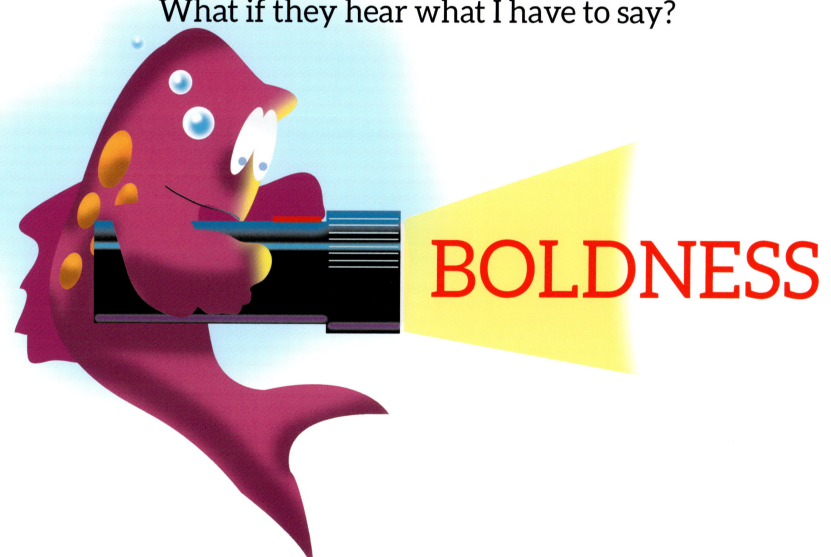

What if?

What if?

What if?

Do you see what we did there?
See how that worked?
Worry turned to wonder
When we switched up the verse.

And there's more we can do. More we can say!
Additional tricks to send worry away!

Some may be serious. Others, more silly!
But they really do work.
"Really?" Really!

When I'm hungry, I eat. When thirsty, I drink.
When I'm tired, I sleep. My eyes tingle? I blink.

So what do we do when anxiety sets in?
What do we do with the ringing within?
When nothing else works and our heads start to spin?

One thing to try is give worry a name
Name it or draw it. Face it, take aim.

You're in charge, you're in power, conductor of all.
Worry Blob is bad. Make him sit in the hall.

Worry Blob is screaming? Making you tired?
He's not the boss, YOU are! Tell him he's fired.

Send him off on a train!
Hear him chug-chug goodbye!

Make him ride on a pigeon
Off into the sky.

A train? A bird?
That may sound
absurd.
But the perfect idea
can take time,
so let's learn.

If one doesn't work,
try a second. A third!
Keep trying and
trying till you find
the right word.

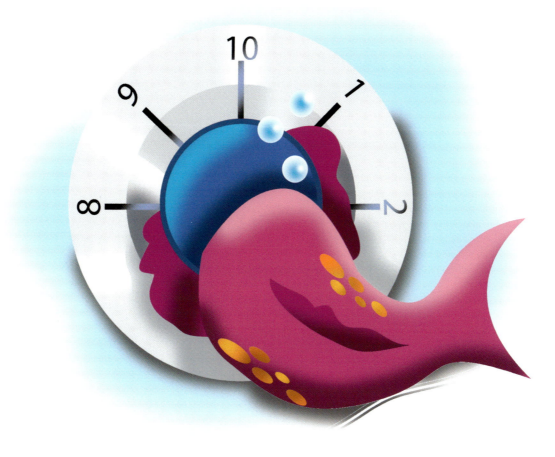

Your brain's a volume dial. Grab it and grin.
When the "What ifs" appear, hold it tight, give a spin.

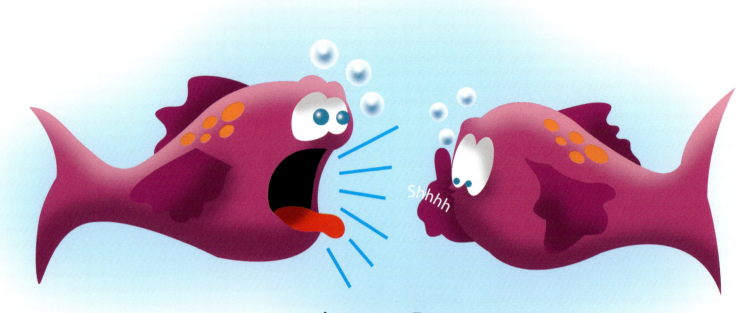

Turn 'em down
Turn 'em down
Turn 'em down, don't delay

From a SCREAM
To a sound
to a whisper, they'll fade.

Let your body relax.
Take a breath, nice and slow.

Try squeezing your hands.
Make them tight, let them go!

But what if a "What if" really happens to you?
What if a "What if" really does come true?

You are resilient.
You have control and grit.
You'll keep going and going and
won't have to quit.

You are resilient.
You can persevere.
There are people who care,
They'll listen, they'll hear.

Do you think every
answer must always
be right?
Even Einstein missed
questions. He was
brighter than bright!

Do you think every try
must end up in a goal?
No one scores every time.
Not even the pros!

Things don't always happen as we might have planned.
We all go off course. We all need a hand.

Don't be scared of the "sometimes"
It can make the day fun!

Routine can be boring.
Blah-blah-blah ho-hum.

Before we end, before we go,
There's one last thing you need to know.

If your Worry Alarm still continues to ring,
And you feel like you need help controlling the thing,

Ask someone to help you! Someone who cares.
A teacher, a parent, somebody aware
Of the ways to help you feel the best you can be.
When you quiet the worry,
you'll set yourself free.

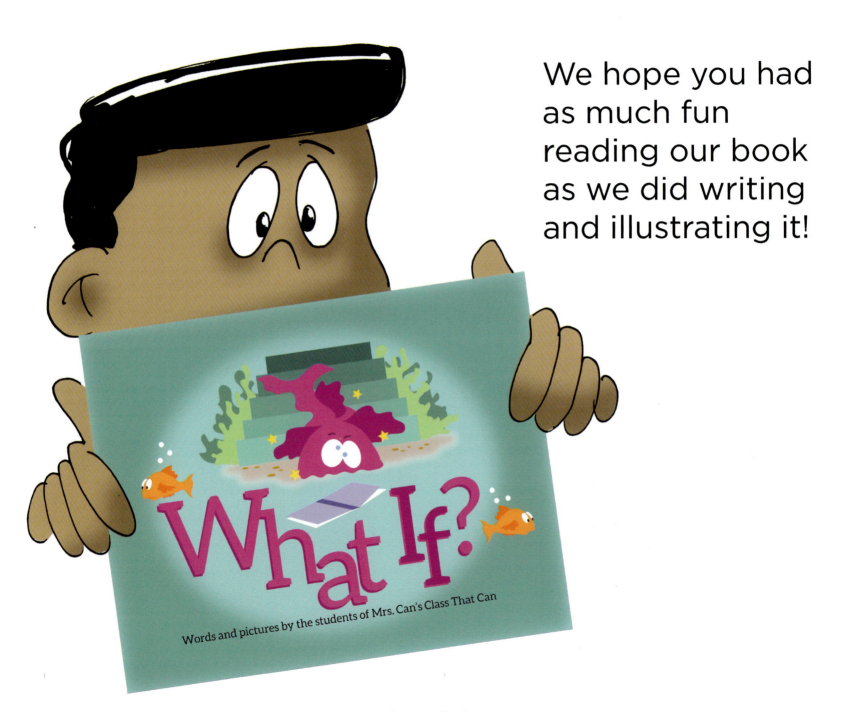

We hope you had as much fun reading our book as we did writing and illustrating it!

Just remember, don't be embarrassed if your Worry Alarm keeps ringing. You now know some tips to control it and, if needed, you know to reach out to an adult who can help.

In The Land of Can, we can all help each other...

STAY HEALTHY!

PAGE 62

Riya Jain

Riya Jain is in 10th grade in Chicago, IL. She authored all the books in *The Class That Can Stay Healthy* series along with empowerment tools for schools across the nation. She has appeared in multiple videos educating young people on health issues. Riya enjoys playing tennis and basketball along with writing poetry, working in student government, and painting.

Riya believes in developing a "CAN mindset" so people can begin to see all of their strengths over deficits, leading to a happier, healthier life!

Bill Dussinger

Bill is an award-winning graphic designer, illustrator and educator from Lititz, PA. He has a BS degree in Art Education from Kutztown University. Bill has been in the design business for over 30 years for many clients such as Discovery Channel, the Oakland Raiders, East Coast Music Hall of Fame and Hershey Entertainment and Resorts. He currently teaches graphic design and illustration at Pennsylvania College of Art & Design in Lancaster, PA. In his spare time he loves to visit his four grandchildren, paint watercolor paintings and watch college football. Penny Lane Graphics, www.plgraphics.com.

Jamison "JJ" Vulopas

With an approach that educators have called transformational, JJ inspires young people to become "Citizens of Can" by embracing the 14 Can Words. His empowerment resources and presentations are used by educators and pediatricians nationwide. JJ is the author of *Land of Can*, *13 Can Words*, *TLoc*, & *The Class That Can Stay Healthy* series. An assistant vice president at Lucid Management and Capital Partners LP, JJ is a 2019 graduate of the Wharton School of the University of Pennsylvania. He lives in New York City.

Mrs. Can

Mrs. Can CAN teach! Mrs. Can is the ultimate teacher, the one who inspires and empowers and compels every one of her students to be the best versions of themselves. In Mrs. Can's class, every child is accepted, appreciated, acknowledged and cared for. Not just for one day. Every day.

By introducing her students to the 14 Words of Can, and by following the tenets outlined in the Can Constitution, Mrs. Can knows that she is creating a classroom of life-long leaders, a classroom where students will define themselves by their cans, look out for each other, and, ultimately, soar!

While writing The Class That Can: Anxiety, *Riya and JJ consulted a licensed clinical psychologist, who provided them with accurate information for the book. Thank you to Lisa Lombard, Ph.D., for adding your expertise to the book and for empowering young people to live in the Land Of Can!*

Lisa Lombard

Lisa Lombard, PhD is a licensed clinical psychologist in private practice in Chicago Illinois, with over 30 years of direct service, teaching, and supervisory experience. She integrates mind-body skills in her therapeutic work with children, families, and adults as they cope with anxiety, stress-mediated health concerns, and pain. She also treats children and adults experiencing unexpected grief and loss. For over 10 years she delivered services within a preschool and elementary school, in addition to her private practice. This was an opportunity to work directly with children in a school setting and to provide parent guidance, clinical supervision to trainees, and consultation on topics such as risk behaviors, trauma, SEL, and screen-time to educators.

In 2020 she joined Northwestern University Feinberg School of Medicine, Department of Medical Social Sciences, Center for Food Allergies and Asthma Research, as a Research Assistant Professor. She applies her knowledge of stress management skills (like mindfulness, hypnosis, and guided imagery) to better understand and meet the psycho-emotional needs of those with food allergies, eczema, and atopic disease. She leads behavioral health initiatives within the Center (combining curated digital behavioral health tips and mindfulness practices).

She earned her B.A. in Behavioral Sciences and her Ph.D. in Psychology/Human Development from the University of Chicago. She completed her externship training at Michael Reese Hospital and an APA-approved internship at the Illinois State Psychiatric Institute in Chicago. She is a licensed clinical psychologist in Illinois and PsyPact Authorized (telehealth across states). She is an ASCH Approved Consultant in hypnosis. She is an active leader in her field, serving as President of the Board of Directors of the National Pediatric Training Institute, a member of the Council of Representatives of the American Psychological Association, and President of the Chicago Society of Clinical Hypnosis. Throughout the pandemic she has provided free weekly virtual mindfulness sessions for her community and colleagues.

Though written by young adults, each book in The Class That Can: Stay Healthy *series is reviewed by a team of doctors that ensures the accuracy of all medical information. The CAN Medical Review Team is led by Dr. Ruchi Gupta, whose dedication inspires young people everywhere to live in the Land of Can!*

Ruchi Gupta

- *Professor of Pediatrics and Medicine, Northwestern Feinberg School of Medicine*
- *Clinical Attending, Ann & Robert H. Lurie Children's Hospital of Chicago*
- *Director, Center for Food Allergy & Asthma Research*

Ruchi Gupta, MD, MPH, has 17 years of experience as a board-certified pediatrician and health researcher and serves as the founding director of the Center for Food Allergy & Asthma Research (CFAAR) at Northwestern University Feinberg School of Medicine and Ann & Robert H. Lurie Children's Hospital of Chicago.

She completed her undergraduate and medical education at the University of Louisville and completed her medical residency at Children's Hospital & Regional Medical Center, University of Washington in Seattle. She completed her pediatric health services research fellowship at Boston Children's Hospital and Harvard Medical School, and went on to receive her Master of Public Health from the Harvard School of Public Health.

Dr. Gupta is world-renowned for her groundbreaking research in food allergy and asthma epidemiology, most notably for her research on the prevalence of pediatric and adult food allergy in the United States. She has also significantly contributed to academic research in the areas of food allergy prevention, socioeconomic disparities in care, and the daily management of these conditions. To reduce the burden of these conditions and improve health equity, she and her team develop, evaluate and disseminate interventions for families and conduct work to inform local, national, and international health policy.

Dr. Gupta is the author of the *Food Allergy Experience* and *Food Without Fear*, has written and co-authored more than 150 peer-reviewed research manuscripts, and has had her work featured on major TV networks and in print media. She speaks to a global audience to share her research with experts and families, and as a physician, food allergy researcher, and food allergy mom, her driving passion is to improve the lives of children and their families through discovery, clinical care, outreach, and education.

Celebrate Health, Empowerment & Safety with our CAN Catalog!

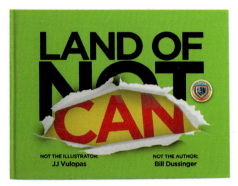

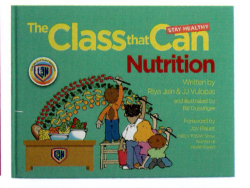

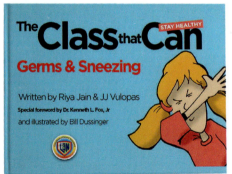
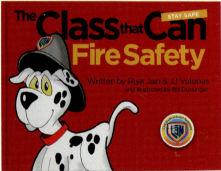
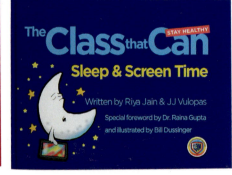

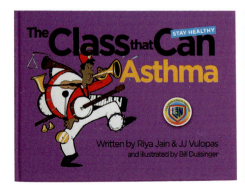
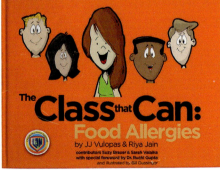
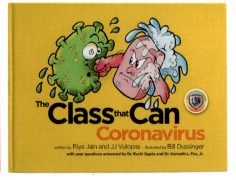

Scan to visit www.thelandofcan.com